W9-AUY-130

HATE THAT CAT

ALSO BY SHARON CREECH

WALK TWO MOONS

ABSOLUTELY NORMAL CHAOS

PLEASING THE GHOST

CHASING REDBIRD

BLOOMABILITY

THE WANDERER

LOVE THAT DOG

A FINE, FINE SCHOOL

RUBY HOLLER

GRANNY TORRELLI MAKES SOUP

HEARTBEAT

REPLAY

SHARON CREECH

HATE THAT CAT

SCHOLASTIC INC.
New York Toronto London Auckland Sydney
Mexico City New Delhi Hong Kong Buenos Aires

ISBN-13: 978-0-545-16597-6
ISBN-10: 0-545-16597-0

12 11 10 9 8 7 6 5 4 3 2 1 9 10 11 12 13 14/0

Printed in the U.S.A. 23

First Scholastic printing, April 2009

For

all you cat lovers out there

and

all you cat haters, too

With special thanks to

Walter Dean Myers

Christopher Myers

Joanna Cotler

Karen Nagel

Alyson Day

and to all the poets

and Mr.-and-Ms. Stretchberrys

who inspire students every day

JACK

ROOM 204—MISS STRETCHBERRY

SEPTEMBER 12

I hate that cat
like a dog hates a rat
I said I hate that cat
like a dog hates a rat

Hate to see it in the morning
hate to see that
F A T black cat.

SEPTEMBER 13

Sorry
I didn't know
you liked cats.
Didn't know
you have one.

SEPTEMBER 14

More poetry?
You probably think
we will remember
what we learned
last year, right?

What if we *don't* remember?
What if our brains shrunk?
What if it's too hard?

But I am glad
you are my teacher
again.
I hope you will
keep moving up
a grade
every year
along with me.

You understand
my
brain.

SEPTEMBER 19

No, I can't write any more
about my dog Sky.
Maybe all of the words
about Sky
flew out of my head
last year.

I *think* about him
all the time
and I *see* him
in my mind
and some of his yellow fur
is still on my yellow chair
and sometimes I think
I hear him
uh-rum, uh-rum
that sound he made
when he was happy.

But no, I can't write about Sky
a-n-y-m-o-r-e.
Maybe I could write about
a cat
a mean cat
a crazy mean fat black cat.

Although . . . my uncle Bill
who is a teacher
in a college
said those words I wrote
about Sky
were NOT poems.
He said they were just
words
coming
out
of
my
head
and that a poem has to rhyme

and have regular meter
and SYMBOLS and METAPHORS
and onomoto-something and
alliter-something.

And I wanted
to
punch
him.

SEPTEMBER 21

Another thing Uncle Bill said
was that my lines should be
l - o - n - g - e - r
like in *real writing*

But here is what happens when I try to
make them longer the page is too wide and
the words get all mumble jumbled and it
makes my eyes hurt all that white space the
edge of the page so far away and in order to
get all the words down that are coming out
of my head I have to forget the commas and
periods or I have to go back and stick, them
in, all over, the place, like this, which
looks, if you ask me, stupid, but if you write
short lines, a person knows where to
breathe, short or long, and I hate to read,
those long lines, and I don't want, to write
them, either.

September 26

I wish you would tell
my uncle Bill
all those things you said today
about our own rhythms
and our own IMAGES
bouncing around in our words
and making them POEMS.

And yes I understand
that if I am ever the
President of the United States
I might be expected to write
very very long lines
but in the meantime
I can make my lines
short
short
short
if I want to.

But even if you told
my uncle Bill
all that stuff
he wouldn't believe you.
He likes to argue.

My mother likes my
short
lines.
She runs her fingers
down them
and then
taps
her lips
once, twice.

And I think I understood
what you said about
onomoto-something
and alliter-something
not HAVING to be

in a poem
and how sometimes
they ENRICH a poem
but sometimes
they can also make a poem
sound *purple.*

Purple!
Ha ha ha.

October 3

Okay, okay, okay
I will learn how to spell
ALLITERATION
and
ONOMATOPOEIA
(right?)
and I will practice them
just in case I ever
need them
to ENRICH
something.

Ready?

Um.

Um.

I can't do it.
Brain frozen.

First you need to have
something to write about.
You can't just
alliterate
and
onomatopoeiate
all over the place
can you?

OCTOBER 10

I felt like there were
feathers in my brain
when you brought out those
objects
and we practiced doing
ALLITERATION
on them
like with the
purple **p**ickle
and the
polished **p**encil
and the
chocolate **ch**alk

but

the pickle was not purple
and the pencil was not polished
and the chalk was not chocolate

so
my uncle Bill would probably say
we are WRONG

even though it is fun
to imagine
a purple pickle
a polished pencil
and chocolate chalk.

October 12

Something I am wondering:
if you cannot hear
do words have no sounds
in your head?

Do you see
a
    silent
        movie?

October 16

So much depends
upon
a red wheel
barrow . . .

The wheelbarrow poem *again*?
Did you forget we read it last year?

Okay, here's one:

So much depends upon
a creeping cat
crouched in the tree
beside the yellow bus stop.

(I bet you're going to ask me
"*Why* does so much depend upon
a creeping cat?"
Right?

Remember:
the wheelbarrow guy
didn't say why
so much depended upon
the red wheelbarrow and
those white chicky chickens.)

OCTOBER 17

ONOMATOPOEIA
made my ears frizzle
today.

All that *buzz buzz buzz*
and
pop! pop!
and
drip and *tinkle* and *trickle*—
the sounds are still
buzzing and popping
in my head.

And the bells bells bells
in that poem you read
by Mr. Poe
(is he alive?)
all those bells bells bells
all those tinkling and jingling

and swinging and ringing
and rhyming and chiming
and clanging and clashing
and tolling and rolling
all those bells bells bells
and that tintinnabulation
what a word!
Tintinnabulation!

I only understood about half
the words in that poem
but like you said
sometimes that is okay
because we *felt* all those
bells
and we *heard* all those
bells
crazily ringing in their
tintinnabulation!

But I bet my uncle Bill
wouldn't like Mr. Poe's
bell poem.
My uncle Bill would probably say
that Mr. Poe repeats himself too much
and needs to find a synonym for *bells*
but I don't care
I love all those bells bells bells.

I thought of some more
onomatopoeia words:
gurgle
burble
wiggle.

Are those right?

And what about
purr purr purr?

And did your cat
really have kittens?
I don't really like
creepy cats.

You should get
a delightful dog.

October 18

Something I am wondering:
if you cannot hear
what happens when you read
purr purr purr
or *gurgle*
or *chocolate chalk*?

Can you somehow
feel
the *purr purr purr*
the *gurgle*
the *chocolate chalk*?

Do you *feel* the sounds
instead of
hear them?

October 19

The Yips

(Inspired by Mr. Edgar Allan Poe)

by Jack

Hear the dogs with their yips
squeaky yips!
What a funny squeaking sound
coming from their lips!
How they ripple ripple ripple
in the shadow of a pickle
In the yipyipabulation
through the air
from the yip yip yip yip
yip yip yip
from the squeaking and the rippling
of the yips.

(P.S. I'm not quite sure how that pickle got in there.)

October 22

If you could not hear
you wouldn't hear
all those funny *yip yip yip*s
but you could *see* the dog
bouncing his head up and down
his mouth flapping
and maybe you would get the idea
that he was making
the same sound
over and over.
Maybe.
But how would you even know
what
        sound
                is?

October 24

I like Maggie's *buzz* poem
you put on the board
on that orange paper
and yes
you can put my *yip* poem
up there
and you can put
my name on it
too.

In my head are so many
bells and buzzes and yips
all jingling and clanking around
bumping into each other.

Very noisy in my head.

If you cannot hear
it must be so
quiet
in your head.

How are your purr purr kittens?
I would write a *purr* poem
except that I don't really like
C
A
T
S.

November 13

When you read that kitten poem
by Miss Valerie Worth
(is she alive?)
I could see that black kitten
dancing sidewise and leaping
and crouching with
her eyes round as oranges
and I could see that black kitten
pouncing with her cactus claws
on a piece of fluff.
It made me laugh,
that black kitten.

It reminded me of my dog Sky
how he would dance around
a skittering leaf
as if it were alive
and he would cock his head
and wag his tail

and scoot backwards
and then yip and pounce
on the fluttery leaf.

He made me laugh, that Sky.

And I hate to admit it
but the kittens you brought
to class
were not creepy.

I'm not saying
I like cats
(dogs are much much better)
but those kittens
were **f**antastically **f**unny
the way they were
skittering around
and *purrrrrrrrr*ing.

I guess I never saw
a kitten up close before
only big **c**reepy **c**ats
that look like they would
love to scratch you.

November 20

I told my dad
about those furry kittens
you brought in to school
and he asked me
if I would like one
and I said
no no no no no.

He is coming to parent conferences
tonight
and I just wanted you to know
that I said
no no no no no.

November 21

Why?
Because kittens grow up
to be *cats*
and what do cats do?

Do they play ball with you
or jump up on you
and lick your face
all slobbery kissy
to show you
they love love love you?

I know one fat black cat
(I hate that cat)
who is meaner than mean
(I hate that cat).

And besides
even if you had a nice cat

that you loved
it might run outside
and into the street
and get
squished
by a car
going *fast*
with many many miles to go
before it sleeps.

Or it could get
sick
really really sick
and never get better.

Or it could
run away
or
get lost

and end up
somewhere
else.

I hope I did not hurt
your feelings
but cats are cats
and dogs are dogs.

P.S. Thank you for saying
nice things about me
to my dad last night.
He liked my *yip* poem
up on the wall
and he likes you, too.
(For true.
I am not just saying that
to make you feel good.)

P.S.S. No I cannot write
about my mother.
That would be
IM-POSS-I-BLE.

November 27

Yes, I know
that all those bad things
could happen to a dog, too,
which is why
I
don't
want
a
dog
either.

I already had
a dog
my dog Sky
my funny furry
smiling dog Sky.

NOVEMBER 30

It's strange that now
when you read a poem to the class
I hear alliteration popping out
everywhere.
I never heard it before
or maybe I heard the sounds
but I didn't know why they were
sticking in my head.

Yesterday after you read the eagle poem
by Mr. Tennyson
(is he alive?)
those first two lines stuck stuck stuck
in my head:

He clasps the crag with crooked hands
Close to the sun in lonely lands . . .

And I could see that eagle

all day long
clasping the crag with his crooked hands
in those lonely lands
just sitting up there watching
watching
before he

F
A
L
L
S

boom like a thunderbolt!

Does he swoop into the sea
and snatch a fish?
Or a little mousie on the hillside?
Or a creepy cat?

Sorry. Just kidding.

DECEMBER 4

THE DOG

(INSPIRED BY MR. TENNYSON)

BY JACK

He pats the kitten with puffy paws
near the window draped with gauze
and yawns and opens up his jaws.

The wrinkled rug beneath him lies.
He watches with his big black eyes
and like a lazy boy he sighs.

Well.
At least the dog
did not
EAT
the kitten.

December 6

Those kittens of yours
surprised me
they got so big
and they are so funny
(especially for cats)

and that black one
with the white spot
on her forehead
she fell asleep
right in my lap
even though I didn't
pet her
well, only a tiny bit

and she was *purrrrrrr*ing
while she slept
so I think she was happy

but
don't get me wrong
a dog is still much better
than a cat.

December 11

The Red-Headed Mailman
(Inspired by Mr. William Carlos Williams)
by Jack

So much depends upon
a red-headed mailman
walking up the drive
holding a blue postcard.

Did you BELIEVE
the postcard I brought in?
Did you BELIEVE
that Mr. Walter Dean Myers—
my all-time favorite poet
who visited our class
last year—
that Mr. Walter Dean Myers
himself
sent me a postcard?

I didn't believe it
when I saw it.
I sat right down on the steps
and read it about fifty times.

And do you BELIEVE
That he mentioned his
C A T ????
His CAT !

I love that postcard
love love love it
but I'm still a little surprised
that Mr. Walter Dean Myers
has a CAT.
I thought he would have
a dashing dog
or maybe a hearty horse.

It is hard to picture
Mr. Walter Dean Myers
with
a
CAT.

December 13

Yes
I wrote back to
Mr. Walter Dean Myers.

I asked him
why he likes his
CAT
so much.

I asked him
if he ever thought about
getting
a
DOG.

DECEMBER 14

THE BAD BLACK CAT

I was standing at the
yellow bus stop
minding my own business
when I heard
mew mew mew
like it was coming from the sky
mew mew mew
and I looked up and saw
a big black cat
all fluffy fur and green eyes
crouched in the tree
mew mew mew
and I thought it was stuck
and so I climbed up the tree
way up high
to the skinny branches
and I leaned way out

and the bus was coming
and I leaned out farther
and grasped the black tail
of that black cat
and I was so glad I'd caught it
I was going to save it
and it would be so relieved
and grateful
and the bus was coming
and that fat black cat
leaped BACKWARDS
onto my head
and it scratched my ears
and my neck
and my face
and it hissed the most awful
spitting horrible *hisssss*
as it scratch scratch scratched
with claws as sharp as needles

and I was bleeding all over the place
and the cat scrambled across my back
and onto my legs
and
d
o
w
n
the tree
while I lay there
clinging to the branch
stinging and bleeding
and the bus
passed
right on by.

I hate that cat.

December 17

Why did the man
throw the cat
out the window?

He wanted to hear
it say
"Me-OW!"

(I made that up.
I thought it was very funny
but maybe you won't like it.
I will try to stop saying
mean things
about ~~mean~~ cats.)

DECEMBER 18

I thought you were kidding
when you said that
Mr. Walter Dean Myers'
grown-up *son* Christopher
had written a book called
Black Cat!

I felt like
Mr. Walter Dean Myers'
whole family
must be in my brain.

When you started reading the book—

> *Black cat, black cat*
> *cousin to the concrete*
> *creeping down our city streets . . .*

—I thought it was going to be about
a mean cat

like the mean black cat
that attacked me.

All the words were
singing in my head
and I was thinking
Wow, that Mr. Christopher Myers
knows about alliteration!

And it turned out not to be
a mean cat.
It was a sauntering and sipping
and dancing and ducking cat
wandering through the city streets
just like a kid
roaming
          and
             poking
                    around.

December 19

I read *Black Cat* to my mother
tapping my fingers
in the rhythm
like you showed us:
HARD-soft HARD-soft
slow and then faster.

She drew a circle with her finger
which means *again*
so I read it over, tapping

and then she put her hand up:
Stop
and I watched while she tapped
the same rhythm

as

she

turned

the

pages

HARD-soft HARD-soft
slow and then faster
and then she closed the book
and tapped her heart
HARD-soft HARD-soft
slow and then faster.

December 20

When you put up that one line
from the eagle poem—

He clasps the crag with crooked hands

—and used all those different colored chalks
to show how Mr. Tennyson
managed to cram in
ALLITERATION
and
ASSONANCE
and
CONSONANCE
all in one line
well
I was impressed
but that doesn't mean
I remember which is which
and

I will never be able to do all that stuff
that Mr. Tennyson does
and did he know he was doing it
when he did it?

I feel stupid.
I am a bad writer.
I'm going to quit.

December 21

Thank you for telling me
I could FORGET
those confusing words
and that it isn't knowing the words
that *describe* writing
that is important—
it is the thoughts in our heads
that are most important
and that *feeling* the rhythm
is even more
wondrous
than *hearing* the rhythm.

And
thank you for saying
I am a genius
(even though I know
you are exaggerating).

January 3

The Gift

(Inspired by Mr. William Carlos Williams)

by Jack

So much depends upon
a black kitten
in a straw basket
under the Christmas tree.

JANUARY 4

My parents woke me
so early
and seemed in a hurry
to rush me downstairs
to the Christmas tree blinking
and
the fire crackling

and I didn't see it right away
that little straw basket
tucked to one side

I was on the floor
pawing through the packages
when something moved—
I thought maybe it was a mouse
that had crept inside

and I jumped back
(not that I am afraid of
a mouse
but it wouldn't be my
favorite thing
to encounter in a pile of presents)
—and then I saw
a blur of black fur—
and I thought
Oh no!
No no no no!
It's the fat black cat!

But then:
a pink nose
tiny black paws
and blinking sleepy eyes

a small black fur ball
not a BIG fat fur ball

a kitten
stumbling
out of the basket
and wobbling over to me
and crawling up on my lap
and licking my pajamas
and I forgot
that I hate cats
as it crawled up onto my chest
and *purrrrrr*ed
and I was smiiiiiling
all
over
the
place.

January 8

So Much

(Inspired by Mr. William Carlos Williams)

by Jack

So much depends upon
a black kitten
dotted with white
beside the photo
of my yellow dog.

JANUARY 10

My ______ is like a _______.

I couldn't think
of a simile.

Brain broken.

Can't even think of a name
for the bouncing black kitten
that's how broken my brain is.

I call her Kitty and Mooshie
and Wiggles and Flopper
but I don't have a real name
for her yet.
Don't tell anyone those goofy
names I use, okay?
They are embarrassing.

January 14

"The Naming of Cats"
by Mr. T. S. Eliot
made me laugh.

Munkustrap? Bombalurina?
Jellyrum???

That Mr. T. S. Eliot
(is he alive?)
must like cats.
And do you think it is
true
that cats have their own
secret names
that only they know—
their "ineffable effable"
names?

Okay, I will unfreeze my brain
now
and write a simile
but I am warning you:
it might not be too good.

The chair in my room
is like a pleasingly plump momma.

JANUARY 17

Go on?
Tell *why* that chair
is like a pleasingly plump momma?
Hmmmm.

The chair in my room
is like a pleasingly plump momma
big and squishy
with stuffing poking out.

It is over there in the corner
sitting quietly
silently
waiting for me
to come and jump
in her lap
and bring
a book or two

or a blanket
when I'm sick.

That plump momma chair
just sits there
waiting for me
and while she waits
she looks a little lonely
to tell you the truth.

She used to have a dog
to jump into her lap
when I wasn't home
but all that is left
of my good yellow dog
are pieces of his fur
stuck here and there.

And now there is a kitten
but the kitten doesn't like
the yellow chair
half as much
as she likes
my pillow.

JANUARY 24

After tremendous tugging
at my broken brain
I finally dug up a **metaphor.**

It's about the kitten
(who now has a name:
Skitter McKitter
because that's what she does
skitter here
skitter there
skitter every-every-where).

Ready? For the metaphor?

THE BLACK KITTEN

The black kitten
is a poet
L E A P I N G
from
line
to
line
sometimes runningrapidly
sometimes s o o t h i n g s l o w l y
here and there
up
and
down

d

o UP

w UP

n UP

and

in a silent steady rhythm

exploring

all

the

tiny

pieces

of

the

world.

January 31

Well, no
don't put it on the board
because now that I read it again
it doesn't make sense.

I know what I was *trying* to say
But I didn't get it right.
The kitten *is* a poet
it's something I *feel*
but I can't get it into words.

A good poet would be able
to paint, with words,
things that you can feel
but don't know how to say.
It's sort of like when
my mother
puts one hand on my back
and one hand on my chest

to *hear* me laughing
or to *feel* me laughing
because
then she understands
what my laughing
sounds like and feels like.

She can see me laugh
and she can sign the word for
laugh
but she cannot hear the laugh.
Yesterday, she put one hand
on Skitter's back
and one hand on her stomach
so she could *hear* the purr.

I cannot explain a purr
just like I cannot explain
why the kitten is a poet
but

she
is

And I cannot explain
how my mother paints
words
with
        her
                hands
but
she
does

And I cannot explain
how—
when we paint words
with each other—
I hear sounds
but I do not know
if she hears anything—

any strange or amazing
or good or terrible
or sparkling or fizzing
sound
at
all.

FEBRUARY 7

So much depends upon

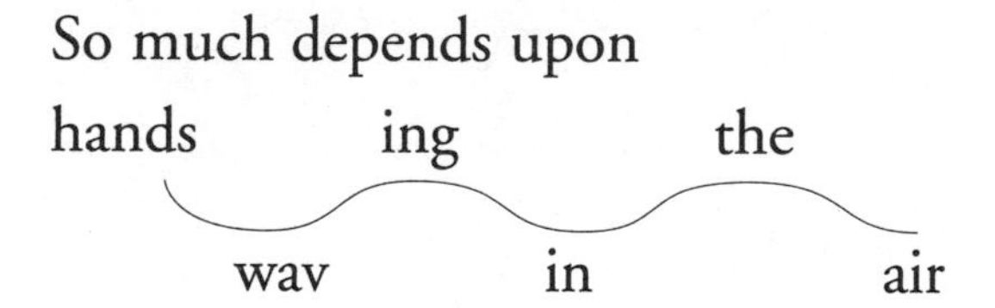

making words
without
sounds

FEBRUARY 11

MY YELLOW CHAIR
by Jack

low chair yellow chair yellow chair yello
yellow chair yellow chair yellow chair yello
squishy soft squishy soft squishy soft squish
squishy soft little hole squishy soft squishy
squishy soft little hole squishy soft squishy
rounded squish squish squish silent *rounded*
arm arm squishy soft squishy soft squishy *arm arm*
arm arm squishy soft black fur squishy soft *arm arm*
arm arm squishy soft yellow fur squishy *arm arm*
arm arm seat squish seat squish black fur *arm arm*
arm arm seat squishy seat squishy seat *arm arm*
squishy seat squishy seat yellow fur squishy seat
silent silent silent silent silent silent silent silent
leg leg leg leg
leg leg leg leg
leg leg leg leg

FEBRUARY 14

Happeeeee Valentine's Day!

I liked when you said
we could try
turning the metaphors
upside down or inside out
and I liked when you used
my chair poem as an example
so
instead of saying
the chair is like a pleasingly plump momma
we could try
my momma is like a pleasingly plump chair

except that now
everyone thinks
my mother is very plump
and looks like a chair

and it doesn't mean the same
when you turn them around
because while the chair
is a lot like a plump momma
my own mother
is like
so
much
more
than a chair.

FEBRUARY 21

Well, okay, I will try it.
Here goes:

My mother is like a plump chair
all squishy soft and huggy
when you sit in her lap
(Just so you know:
I am too old to sit in her lap.
I'm just saying this for the poem.)

Her arms hold you in
so you won't fall
and will feel
safe

And she has sturdy legs
(although I want to make it clear

that my real mother has two legs
not four)
and a straight back

She is proud
but not too proud
and she is there
waiting for me
always
quietly
waiting
for
me.

End of Poem.

So here's the problem:
My real mother

can't always be
waiting for me
because she works at night
and my mother
doesn't sit in the same place
day in and day out
like a chair does—
she is always
moving moving moving
her hands

wav air

ing the

in

talking to us

with hands

those

and she isn't plump at all
and like I said
she has two legs, not four
and so
really
she is not very much
like a chair
at
all.

I will never be
a
real
poet.

FEBRUARY 25

Today the fat black cat
up in the tree by the bus stop
dropped a nut on my head
thunk
and when I yelled at it
that fat black cat said
Murr-mee-urrr
in a
nasty
spiteful
way.

I hate that cat.

FEBRUARY 28

I am getting
a little worried
about poor
Mr. William Carlos Williams
(is he alive?)

I mean:
first there was the
poem about the
red wheelbarrow
and the chicky chickens
and it's true I like that poem now
(it grows on you)
but
those two poems about the
PLUMS . . . !!!???

I think Kaitlyn was crying
because she felt stupid

and to tell you the truth
I felt stupid, too,
because even though
those were nice little thingies
that Mr. William Carlos Williams said
about the sweet plums
and the old lady
and even though I could see
little pictures
in my mind
when you were reading
the plum poems
it would be very very hard
to explain to my uncle Bill
why those are poems
and not little notes
scribbled on scrap paper.

And did you notice that
Mr. William Carlos Williams
does NOT use much in the way of
ALLITERATION
or
ONOMATOPOEIA
or
SIMILE
or
METAPHOR?
Mm? Did you notice that?

March 6

This morning I left
a note
for my mother:

THIS IS JUST TO SAY

I have eaten
the pudding
that was in
the fridge

and which
you were maybe
saving
for dessert

Forgive me
it was so yum
so thick
so creamy

March 7

Those non-poems
of
kookoo Mr. William Carlos Williams
are running in my head:

Mom in the Kitchen

(Inspired by Mr. William Carlos Williams)

by Jack

crunching on a pickle
in the middle of the room
juice running down her arm

It tastes good to her
It tastes good
to her. It tastes
good to her

You can tell by
the way she closes her eyes
and licks her lips
and then her arm

Refreshed
a song of dill pickles
filling the air
It tastes good to her

MARCH 13

You know WHAT?
Today in the library
I found some more poems
by Mr. William Carlos Williams
and do you know what he wrote?

A poem about a cat
A CAT!

The title is POEM
(Is Mr. William Carlos Williams
a little lazy?)
and it is only about
a cat climbing over a jamcloset
(what is a jamcloset?)
and into a flowerpot!

That is IT.
That is the p-o-e-m.

But as soon as I read it
I saw in my head
Skitter McKitter
my black kitten
so
here is a
non-poem
about her:

*Non-Poem**

(Inspired by lazy Mr. William Carlos Williams)

by Jack

As the kitten
leaped over
the pot

of blue violets
first the front
paws

gracefully
then the hind paws
landing

into the bottom of
the kitchen sink

*(Note: if Mr. WCW doesn't have to think of a title, I don't either, right?)

MARCH 14

ANOTHER NON-POEM

(INSPIRED BY MR. WILLIAM CARLOS WILLIAMS)

BY JACK

The fat black cat
crouched on a limb
of the maple tree

needle claws
scratching
the bark

menacingly
then the tail
whacking
at the branch
in warning.

March 21

Just as I expected
my uncle Bill
is not a big fan
of Mr. William Carlos Williams.

Uncle Bill says Mr. WCW
is a "minor poet"
and
a "foe poet"
(later my dad explained
he meant *faux*
which means "fake")
and I said

"What about the
'so much depends upon'
poem
and the plum poems?"

(which are stuck in my head
and I can say them from memory)

and Uncle Bill said
"Tuh! Overrated, highly
overrated!"

And I found myself
sticking up for
poor Mr. William Carlos Williams
and the small ordinary things
he writes about
and the small ordinary moments
that you don't notice
until you read his poems
and Uncle Bill said

"Small things? Small moments?
Tuh! Give me LARGE things!
LARGE moments!
Give me poems about
death and dying
about war and tragedy
and philosophical metaphors
give me sonnets
give me odes . . ."

blah blah blah

The only interesting thing
he said while he was visiting
was that he is allergic to cats
and he sneezed a lot just to
prove it
and he made us lock Skitter McKitter
in my room
and

when he left, my dad said
two things.
First:
"Sometimes I envy your mom
not being able to hear"
and
Second:
"If Uncle Bill
is allergic to cats
maybe he won't be able
to visit us anymore."

Ha ha ha.

MARCH 26

This is just to say that
Skitter McKitter
has run away

And maybe Uncle Bill
would say this is not a
tragedy
but in our house
it
is
a
tragedy.

MARCH 27

How can you go from
hating cats
to loving one cat
in particular
one black cat
one Skitter McKitter cat
who chases a brown nut
across the wood floor
and who trails balls of string
over chairs and under tables
and who falls over backwards
when she is swatting at a plant
and who leaps in your lap
and *purrrrrrrrr*s
and who sleeps on your pillow
curled behind your head
with one paw on your ear
and who crawls under the covers
to nip at your toes

how can you love a little cat
so much
in such a
short
short
time?

March 28

Last night my mother
signed the word C-A-T
and then tapped
her heart
HARD-soft
HARD-soft
HARD-soft.

MARCH 31

Still no Skitter McKitter.
We think she got out
when the plumber
left the door open.
I keep thinking about
Mr. Christopher Myers'
roaming cat
and the person in the poem-story
who says over and over:
where's your home, where do you go?

There is a big
emptiness
in our house
just like there was
when my dog Sky
died.

We've looked everywhere
we've called Skitter's name
we've put out bowls of milk
but the only cat who
slurps the milk
is that other black cat
that mean fat black cat
that scratched me.

I saw it creeping away
from the milk bowl
licking its chin
lazy waddling cat
flicking its proud tail.

I hate that cat.

And more bad news:
yesterday I received a postcard
from Mr. Walter Dean Myers
and on it he said that
his cat
DIED.

He said his cat was old
and had lived a
good
long
life
but that he
misses
his cat.

I know what he means.
Keep your doors
closed
so your cats do not

get
out
and if you have any
old cats
take good care of them.

APRIL 2

Skitter McKitter:
Here is your home.
Why did you go?

April 11

So much depends upon
a black kitten
mewing outside
your back door.

Yes, Skitter McKitter is back!

I heard scratching
and then howling
but it didn't sound like Skitter.

When I opened the door
there was the fat black cat
making a ruckus
and then I heard a
softer mewing
kitten mewing
Skitter mewing
and lying there

beside the door
was Skitter McKitter
looking thin
and bedraggled
with a gash on one ear
and a clump of fur missing
from her neck
and when I went to reach
for Skitter
the fat black cat
put a paw out
protectively
and licked Skitter's ear
and then nudged Skitter
up and into my hands
and then the fat black cat
sat there very still—
silent—
as I carried Skitter inside.

I left the door open
in case the fat black cat
wanted to come inside too
but instead the fat black cat
turned and walked away
whisking its fat black tail
whisk whisk.

I think the fat black cat
found Skitter McKitter
and
saved her
and brought her
home.

I'm sorry I hated that cat.

When I held Skitter
in my lap
and petted her
she licked my hand

she licked it
and licked it
It tasted good to her
It tasted good
to her. It tasted
good
to
her.

APRIL 18

THE KITTEN

(INSPIRED BY MR. ALFRED LORD TENNYSON)

BY JACK

She pats the package with padded paws
and pulls apart the golden gauze
with her tiny furry jaws.

Then like an acrobat she leaps
legs and ribbon in a heap
tangled round and tangled deep.

April 25

The Purr

(Inspired by Mr. Edgar Allan Poe

and my new thesaurus)

by Jack

Hear the kitten with her purr,
humming purr!
What a contagious contentment
her vibrations spur!
How she hum hum hums
keeping time time time
in a sort of thrumming rhyme
To the murmurabulation of the thrums
and the hums
of her purr, purr, purr, purr,
purr, purr, purr—
of the humming and the thrumming
of her purr.

May 2

Thank you thank you thank you
for showing me all the books
of cat poems
and all the books
that tell a story
in
poems.
I never knew
a writer could do that—
tell a whole story
in
poems.

I already read the one
by Mr. Robert Cormier
(alive?)
and next
by my bed is

that dust book by
Ms. Karen Hesse
(alive?)
and underneath that one
is the Essie and Amber one
by Ms. Vera B. Williams
(alive?)
and on my bulletin board
is a list you gave me
of so many poets
whose books I can read
and also on my bulletin board
is the funny poem-picture
of the cat chair
by Mr. Chris Raschka
(alive?)
and that poem
by Mr. Lee Bennett Hopkins
(alive?)
about growing up

to

be

a

writer.

I now have

a treasure of words

in

my

room.

MAY 5

SILENT SOUNDS OF MOM

(INSPIRED BY MR. EDGAR ALLAN POE)

BY JACK

See her hands in the air
waving here waving there!
What flickering formations
those compositions dare!
How she sing sing sings
in a swish and a bound
bringing sound sound sound
To the silence of the air
to the silentabulation of the hush
and the hums
of the air, air, air, air,
air, air, air—
of the humming and the hushing
of the air.

MAY 9

POETS' DAY

It was grandilicious
finding pictures
of so many poets
and putting them
on the wall in our classroom
all those poets
looking back at us
and beside them
some of their poems
so many words
and images in our heads
and although I wish
they were all alive

and that Dwayne hadn't written
DEAD
next to the dead ones
their words are all still
there
waiting
for
someone
to
read
them
those ineffable effable
words
thrumming like
*purrrrrr*ing
in
our
heads.

May 16

Love That Cat

(Inspired by Mr. Walter Dean Myers)

by Jack

Love that cat,
like a bird loves to twitter
I said I love that cat
like a bird loves to twitter
Love to call her in the morning
love to call her
"Hey there, Skitter McKitter!"

May 19

The fat black cat
has been coming to our back door
Moirrrr?
she says
as if asking a question

I pour milk in the bowl
and the fat black cat
slurp slurps
and then sits back
staring at me
her tail slapping slowly
on the ground
shisk shisk

Moirrrr?

Skitter
skitters up
and leaps forward
her front paws
occasionally landing
in the bowl
and
the fat black cat
licks the top
of Skitter's head
and then turns
and saunters away
apparently
satisfied.

May 23

Thank you for saying
more nice things
about me
to my parents
last night
when we read our poems
at school.

My mother doesn't usually
come to these things
because she can't hear
what's going on
but when you said
I could sign for her
this is what she
said (signed) to me:
"I love that Miss Stretchberry."

And although I was embarrassed
to stand up in front of everyone
and sign all those words
for my mother—
too many eyes on me—
and it was very hard
to keep up with everyone
speaking so fast—
when I saw my mother's face
it felt good to me
it felt good to me
it felt good
to
me.

JUNE 5

THIS IS JUST TO SAY

I will listen
for you

I will hear
all the sounds
in the world

all the
delicious
ineffable
effable
sounds

all the
thrumming
and
humming

and

tintinnabulating

sounds

I will hear

all the sounds

in the

world

and I will write them down

so you

can

hear

them

too.

Some of the poems used by Miss Stretchberry

Love That Boy

BY WALTER DEAN MYERS

Love that boy,
like a rabbit loves to run
I said I love that boy
like a rabbit loves to run
Love to call him in the morning
love to call him
"Hey there, son!"

First stanza

Love That Dog

(Inspired by Walter Dean Myers)

by Jack

Love that dog,
like a bird loves to fly
I said I love that dog
like a bird loves to fly
Love to call him in the morning
love to call him
"Hey there, Sky!"

My Yellow Dog

BY JACK

My yellow dog
followed me everywhere
every which way I turned
he was there
wagging his tail
and slobber
coming out
of his mouth
when he was smiling
at me
all the time
as if he was
saying
thank you thank you thank you
for choosing me

and jumping up on me
his shaggy straggly paws
on my chest
like he was trying
to hug the insides
right out of me.

And when us kids
were playing outside
kicking the ball
he'd chase after it
and push it with his nose
push push push
and getting slobber
all over the ball
but no one cared
because he was such
a funny dog
that dog Sky

that straggly furry
smiling
dog
Sky.

And I'd call him
every morning
every evening
Hey there, Sky!

The Red Wheelbarrow

BY WILLIAM CARLOS WILLIAMS

so much depends
upon

a red wheel
barrow

glazed with rain
water

beside the white
chickens.

The Bells

BY EDGAR ALLAN POE

Hear the sledges with the bells,
Silver bells!
What a world of merriment their melody foretells!
How they tinkle, tinkle, tinkle,
In the icy air of night!
While the stars, that oversprinkle
All the heavens, seem to twinkle
With a crystalline delight;
Keeping time, time, time,
In a sort of Runic rhyme,
To the tintinnabulation that so musically wells
From the bells, bells, bells, bells,
Bells, bells, bells—
From the jingling and the tinkling of the bells.

Hear the mellow wedding bells,
Golden bells!
What a world of happiness their harmony foretells!
Through the balmy air of night
How they ring out their delight!
From the molten-golden notes,
And all in tune,
What a liquid ditty floats
To the turtle-dove that listens, while she gloats
On the moon!
Oh, from out the sounding cells,
What a gush of euphony voluminously wells!
How it swells!
How it dwells
On the Future! how it tells
Of the rapture that impels

To the swinging and the ringing
  Of the bells, bells, bells,
Of the bells, bells, bells, bells,
    Bells, bells, bells—
To the rhyming and the chiming of the bells!

First and second stanzas

kitten

BY VALERIE WORTH

The black kitten,
Arched stiff,
Dances sidewise
From behind
The chair, leaps,
Tears away with
Ears back, spins,
Lands crouched
Flat on the floor,
Sighting something
At nose level,
Her eyes round
As oranges, her
Hind legs marking
Time: then she
Pounces, cactus-

Clawed, upon
a strayed
Strand of fluff:
Can anyone
Believe that she
Doesn't ask us
To laugh?

The Eagle

BY ALFRED, LORD TENNYSON

He clasps the crag with crooked hands;
Close to the sun in lonely lands,
Ring'd with the azure world, he stands.

The wrinkled sea beneath him crawls;
He watches from his mountain walls,
And like a thunderbolt he falls.

Black Cat

BY CHRISTOPHER MYERS

black cat, black cat
cousin to the concrete
creeping down our city streets
where do you live, where will we meet?

sauntering like rainwater down storm drains
between cadillac tires and the curb

sipping water from fire hydrants

dancing to the banging beats of passing jeeps

ducking under the red circling of sirens cutting
through the night

in the wake of sunday night families spilling
from blue neon churches

black cat, black cat, we want to know
where's your home, where do you go?

Extract

The Naming of Cats

BY T. S. ELIOT

The naming of cats is a difficult matter,
It isn't just one of your holiday games;
You may think at first I'm mad as a hatter
When I tell you a cat must have three
different names.

First of all, there's the name
that the family use daily,
Such as Victor, or Jonathan,
George or Bill Bailey—
All of them sensible everyday names.
There are fancier names
if you think they sound sweeter,
Some for the gentlemen,
some for the dames;
Such as Plato, Admetus,
Electra, Demeter—
But all of them sensible everyday names.

But I tell you,
a cat needs a name that's peculiar,
A name that is peculiar, and more dignified,
Else how can he
keep up his tail perpendicular,
Or spread out his whiskers,
or cherish his pride?

Of names of this kind,
I can give you a quorum,
Such as Munkustrap, Quazo or Coripat,
Such as Bombalurina, or else Jellyrum—
Names that never belong
to more than one cat.

But above and beyond
there's still one name left over,
And that is the name that you will never guess;
The name
that no human research can discover—

But The Cat Himself Knows,
and will never confess.

When you notice a cat in profound meditation,
The reason, I tell you, is always the same:
His mind is engaged in rapt contemplation
Of the thought, of the thought,
of the thought of his name:
His ineffable effable
Effanineffable
Deep and inscrutable singular Name.

This Is Just to Say

BY WILLIAM CARLOS WILLIAMS

I have eaten
the plums
that were in
the icebox

and which
you were probably
saving
for breakfast

Forgive me
they were so delicious
so sweet
and so cold

To a Poor Old Woman

BY WILLIAM CARLOS WILLIAMS

munching a plum on
the street a paper bag
of them in her hand

They taste good to her
They taste good
to her. They taste
good to her

You can see it by
the way she gives herself
to the one half
sucked out in her hand

Comforted
a solace of ripe plums
seeming to fill the air
They taste good to her

Poem

BY WILLIAM CARLOS WILLIAMS

As the cat
climbed over
the top of

the jamcloset
first the right
forefoot

carefully
then the hind
stepped down

into the pit of
the empty flowerpot

Books on the Class Poetry Shelf

Adedjouma, Davida, ed. *The Palm of My Heart: Poetry by African American Children*, illustrated by Gregory Christie (Lee & Low, 1996).

Adoff, Arnold. *Street Music: City Poems*, illustrated by Karen Barbour (HarperCollins, 1995).

Alarcón, Francisco X. *Iguanas in the Snow and Other Winter Poems/Iguanas en la nieve y otros poemas de invierno*, illustrated by Maya Christina Gonzalez (Children's Book Press, 2001).

Bryan, Ashley. *Sing to the Sun* (HarperCollins, 1992).

Cormier, Robert. *Frenchtown Summer* (Delacorte, 1999).

Eliot, T. S. *Old Possum's Book of Practical Cats*, illustrated by Edward Gorey (Harcourt, 1982).

Esbensen, Barbara Juster. *Swing Around the Sun: Poems*, illustrated by Cheng-Khee Chee, Janice Lee Porter, Mary GrandPré, and Stephen Gammell (Carolrhoda, 2003).

Fleischman, Paul. *Joyful Noise: Poems for Two Voices*, illustrated by Eric Beddows (HarperCollins, 1988).

Frost, Robert. *The Poetry of Robert Frost*, edited by Edward Connery Lathem (Holt, Rinehart, 1969).

George, Kristine O'Connell. *Little Dog Poems*, illustrated by June Otani (Clarion, 1999).

Giovanni, Nikki. *The Sun Is So Quiet*, illustrated by Ashley Bryan (Henry Holt, 1996).

Greenfield, Eloise. *Honey, I Love and Other Love Poems*, illustrated by Diane and Leo Dillon (HarperCollins, 1978).

Greenfield, Eloise. *Night on Neighborhood Street*, illustrated by Jan Spivey Gilchrist (Dial Books, 1991).

Greenfield, Eloise. *Under the Sunday Tree*, paintings by Mr. Amos Ferguson (HarperCollins, 1988).

Grimes, Nikki. *A Pocketful of Poems*, illustrated by Javaka Steptoe (Clarion, 2001).

Hesse, Karen. *Out of the Dust* (Scholastic, 1997).

Hopkins, Lee Bennett. *Been to Yesterdays*, illustrated by Charlene Rendeiro (Wordsong/Boyds Mill, 1995).

Hopkins, Lee Bennett. *Good Rhymes, Good Times*, illustrated by Frané Lessac (HarperCollins, 1995).

Hopkins, Lee Bennett. *Pass the Poetry, Please!* 3rd ed. (HarperCollins, 1998).

Hughes, Langston. *The Dream Keeper and Other Poems*, illustrated by Brian Pinkney (Knopf, 1994).

Janeczko, Paul B., ed. *A Poke in the I*, illustrated by Chris Raschka (Candlewick, 2001).

Janeczko, Paul B., ed. *Stone Bench in an Empty Park*, photographed by Henri Silberman (Orchard, 2000).

Koch, Kenneth. *Rose, Where Did You Get That Red? Teaching Great Poetry to Children* (Vintage Books, 1990).

Kuskin, Karla. *The Sky Is Always in the Sky*, illustrated by Isabelle Dervaux (Laura Geringer/HarperCollins, 1998).

Kuskin, Karla. *Toots the Cat*, illustrated by Lisze Bechtold (Henry Holt, 2005).

Levy, Constance. *Splash! Poems of Our Watery World*, illustrated by David Soman (Orchard, 2002).

Little, Jean. *Hey World, Here I Am!*, illustrated by Sue Truesdell (HarperTrophy, 1990).

Livingston, Myra Cohn, ed. *Cat Poems*, illustrated by Trina Schart Hyman (Holiday House, 1987).

Livingston, Myra Cohn. *Cricket Never Does: A Collection of Haiku and Tanka*, illustrated by Kees de Kiefte (McElderry Books, 1997).

Livingston, Myra Cohn. *I Am Writing a Poem About . . . : A Game of Poetry* (McElderry Books, 1997).

Moore, Geoffrey, ed. *The Penguin Book of American Verse* (Penguin, 1983).

Myers, Christopher. *Black Cat* (Scholastic, 1999).

Myers, Walter Dean. *Brown Angels: An Album of Pictures and Verse* (HarperCollins, 1993).

Nye, Naomi Shihab, ed. *Salting the Ocean: 100 Poems by Young Poets*, illustrated by Ashley Bryan (Greenwillow, 2000).

Nye, Naomi Shihab, ed. *The Tree Is Older Than You Are* (Simon & Schuster, 1995).

Sandburg, Carl. *Grassroots: Poems by Carl Sandburg*, illustrated by Wendell Minor (Browndeer, 1998).

Silverstein, Shel. *A Light in the Attic* (HarperCollins, 1981).

Sones, Sonya. *Stop Pretending: What Happened When My Big Sister Went Crazy* (HarperTempest, 2001).

Thomas, Joyce Carol. *Brown Honey in Broomwheat Tea*, illustrated by Floyd Cooper (HarperCollins, 1993).

Williams, Vera B. *Amber Was Brave, Essie Was Smart* (Greenwillow/HarperCollins, 2001).

Woodson, Jacqueline. *Locomotion* (Putnam, 2003).

Worth, Valerie. *all the small poems and fourteen more*, illustrated by Natalie Babbitt (Farrar, Straus and Giroux, 1994).

Yolen, Jane. *Bird Watch: A Book of Poetry*, illustrated by Ted Lewin (Putnam, 1990).